MOM'S NOT Cleanin' Your Room

CAUTION

Author

LIN HAWTHORNE

Illustrator

STEVIE MAHARDHIKA

For our four mess-makers and for my Mimi,
who loved her messy granddaughter anyway

-LH

Hey, what about the DADS?
For all the GREAT dads picking up all the things

-SM

Book TWO in the Mom's Not® Book Series
A Grow With Me® Book

MOM'S NOT Cleanin' Your Room

3+1

THREE PLUS ONE PUBLISHING

PHOENIX

Author
LIN HAWTHORNE

Illustrator
STEVIE MAHARDHIKA

Now that you're big,
(much bigger than small),

there's something
you're ready to know.

Your roost is a wreck—
get on board,
sweep the deck!

BECAUSE...

The pile has grown tall—
it looks ready to fall.

And critters are now moving in!

The packrats unpacked,

and the place is ransacked!

"AN EVICTION IS NEAR...

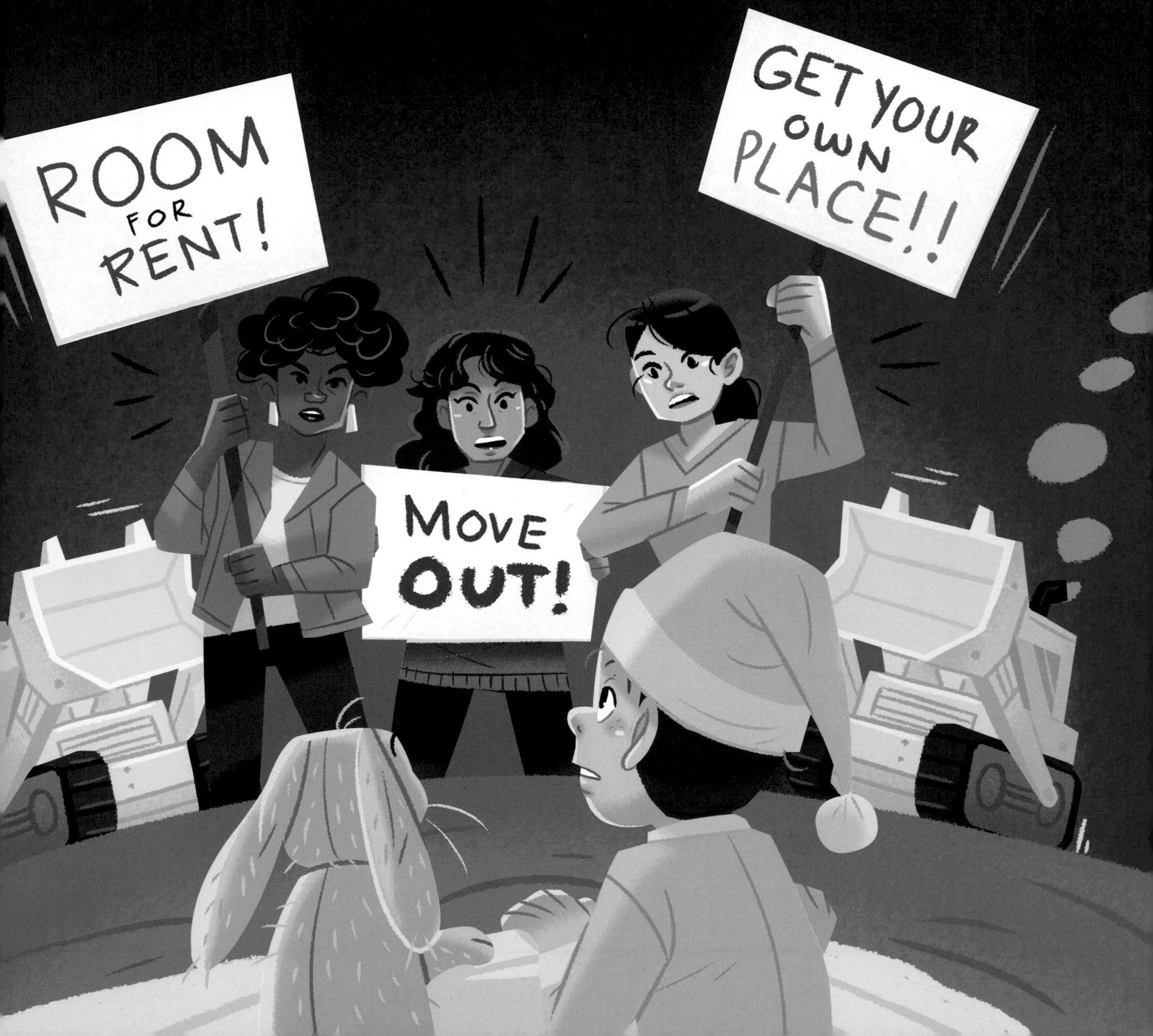

if you don't pick up, dear."

"I know, but there's too much to do!"

"Try one at a time.

Sing a song.

Make it rhyme!"

The dust bunnies sleep tight,
dreaming fuzzy goodnights

Please tell cousin
Abacus that Aunt
Milfred says "hi!"

with blankets of dirt
on their bed.

Now wipe them right down.

Turn their frowns upside down!

The drawers that exploded
need clothing reloaded...

"A RAINBOW OF
OUTFITS GALORE!"

If they fit,

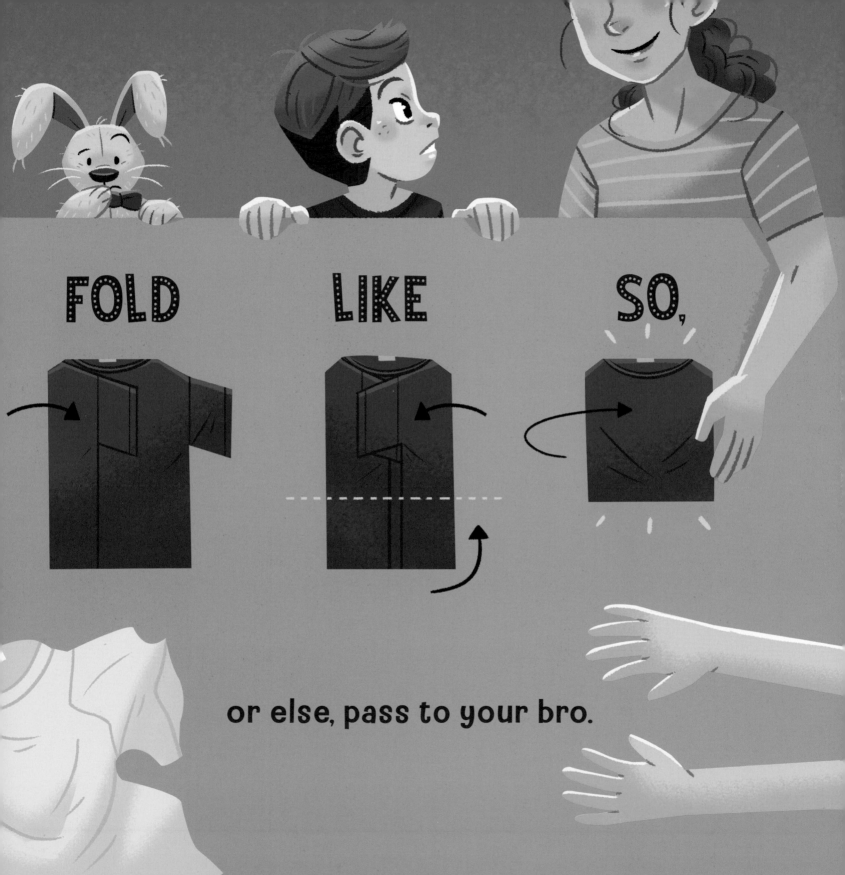

FOLD LIKE SO,

or else, pass to your bro.

It's easy to sleep,
work, relax, and repeat...

in a squeaky clean pen.
"Look, how neat!"

"I'm proud you worked hard—now let's tackle the yard."

"Wait, what's that I see?
Some elbows and knees?

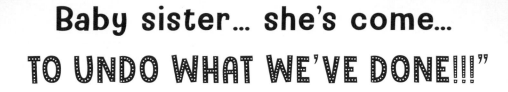

Baby sister... she's come...
TO UNDO WHAT WE'VE DONE!!!"